to: _____

from: _____

Published by Sellers Publishing, Inc.
161 John Roberts Road, South Portland, ME 04106
Visit us at www.sellerspublishing.com • E-mail: rsp@rsvp.com

© 2017 Sellers Publishing, Inc.

Illustrations © 2017 Becca Cahan

All rights reserved.

Managing Editor: Mary L. Baldwin
Production Editor: Charlotte Cromwell

ISBN-13: 978-1-4162-4629-9

Printed and bound in China.

10 9 8 7 6 5 4 3 2 1

SIMPLY 50

CELEBRATE the SIMPLE JOYS of LIFE

art by BECCA ♥ CAHAN

SELLERS
PUBLISHING

All the world is a birthday cake,
so take a piece, but not too much.

— *George Harrison*

TODAY·WE CELEBRATE YOU!

I'd say the best thing about being 50 is that there is a kind of confidence that comes with age. Hopefully, you've made peace with whatever direction your life has taken you, so there is no longer that pressure to have to prove anything to yourself or the world.

— *Susan Seidelman*

It's never too late to create
a vision for helping others and
promoting positive changes.
The reward of philanthropy isn't
recognition, it is the empowerment of
using your voice and your resources
to create change.

— *Lorna Wendt*

AMAZING THINGS CAN HAPPEN

Fifty is an excellent age for reform of all sorts. You have enough experience and good judgment to know something about yourself . . . so, gauging your desires and your strength, you adjust and straighten and balance and alter what needs altering and press on.

— *Garrison Keillor*

You may think 50 is old,
but three years from now
you will think it is young.
That's one very positive
aspect of thinking ahead.

— *Diane von Furstenberg*

·BE· PATIENT WITH·YOURSELF

LIFE IS VERY SHORT & THERE'S NO TIME FOR fussing + fighting MY FRIEND

-JOHN LENNON & PAUL McCARTNEY-

Be patient and understanding.
Life is too short to be
vengeful or malicious.

— *Phillips Brooks*

As I look at turning 50, I can finally say
that I've come to terms with myself. . . .
True beauty is about accepting
and feeling good about who you are.

— *Bobbi Brown*

BELIEVE IN YOURSELF

The Future BELONGS to those WHO BELIEVE in their DREAMS

ELEANOR ROOSEVELT

I have enjoyed greatly
the second blooming —
at the age of 50, say — that a whole
new life has opened before you.

— *Agatha Christie*

Happiness doesn't depend on what we have, but it does depend on how we feel toward what we have. We can be happy with little and miserable with much.

— *William Dempster Hoard*

Good FRIENDS
ARE LIKE
STARS.
YOU DON'T
ALWAYS SEE THEM,
BUT YOU KNOW THEY'RE
Always
THERE.
BECCA CAHAN

What I've found most useful since I've turned 50 is that the things that I feel are deep in my life have gotten deeper. My friendships with the people I really like have become deeper.

— *Wendy Wasserstein*

Take deep breaths and look around you . . . really see, from your innermost being, the flowers, earth, rocks, trees, and sky, the variety of colors, the light that dances on rivers, lakes, leaves, snow, or sea . . . and let that 'light" dance inside of you.

— *Kristina Hurrell*

CULTIVATE light IN YOUR life

be silly
BE HONEST
be kind
RALPH WALDO EMERSON

To get back my youth
I would do anything in the world,
except take exercise, get up early,
or be respectable.

— *Oscar Wilde*

Turning 50 is an enriching experience.
Live moment to moment. Help others
more. Have more fun with them, and
appreciate what is of value.

— *Robert Thurman, Ph.D.*

GROWING · OLD
— is —
MANDATORY.
Growing
up
IS OPTIONAL!

Most people don't grow up. Most people age. They find parking spaces, honor their credit cards, get married, have children and call that maturity. What that is, is aging.

— *Maya Angelou*

By the time we hit 50, we have learned our hardest lessons. We have found out that only a few things are really important. We have learned to take life seriously, but never ourselves.

— *Marie Dressler*

KNOWING YOURSELF is the BEGINNING of all WISDOM

ARISTOTLE

the IMPORTANT THING to YOU is NOT how MANY YEARS in YOUR LIFE, BUT HOW MUCH LIFE IN YOUR YEARS!

EDWARD STIEGLITZ

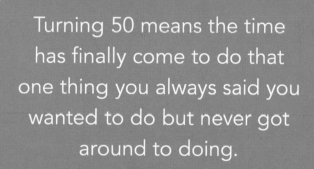

Turning 50 means the time
has finally come to do that
one thing you always said you
wanted to do but never got
around to doing.

— *Luis Santeiro*

At 50, You might finally have some time
to read books more challenging
than summer novels.

— *Robert Thurman, Ph.D.*

time you ENJOY WASTING you is not WASTED TIME

—MARTHE TROLY-CURTIN—

You are never too old
to set another goal
or to dream a new dream.

— Les Brown

Never too late to learn some embarrassingly basic, stupidly obvious things about oneself.

— *Alain de Botton*

Live
IN THE
sunshine
SWIM
in the sea,
DRINK
THE
wild air.

RALPH WALDO EMERSON

A birthday is just the first day
of another 365-day journey
around the sun.
Enjoy the trip.

— *Author Unknown*

Nature gives you the face you have at twenty; it is up to you to merit the face you have at fifty.

– *Coco Chanel*

NOW AND THEN, IT'S GOOD TO PAUSE IN OUR PURSUIT OF HAPPINESS AND JUST BE HAPPY

-GUILLAUME APOLLINAIRE-

You don't stop laughing when you grow old,
you grow old when you stop laughing.

— *George Bernard Shaw*

In terms of days and moments lived, you'll never again be as young as you are right now, so spend this day, the youth of your future, in a way that deflects regret. Invest in yourself. Have some fun. Do something important. Love somebody extra. In one sense, you're just a kid, but a kid with enough years on her to know that every day is priceless."

— *Victoria Moran*

50 years: here's a time when you have to separate yourself from what other people expect of you, and do what you love.

– *Jim Carrey*

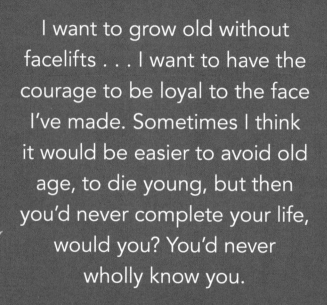

I want to grow old without facelifts . . . I want to have the courage to be loyal to the face I've made. Sometimes I think it would be easier to avoid old age, to die young, but then you'd never complete your life, would you? You'd never wholly know you.

— *Marilyn Monroe*

Not all those who wander are lost

J.R.R. TOLKIEN

Twenty years from now you will be
more disappointed by the things you
didn't do than by the ones you did do.
So throw off the bowlines.
Sail away from the safe harbor.
Catch the trade winds in your sails.
Explore. Dream. Discover.

— *Mark Twain*

I've enjoyed every age I've been and each has had its own individual merit. Every laugh line, every scar, is a badge I wear to show I've been present, the inner rings of my personal tree trunk that I display proudly for all to see.

— *Pat Benatar*

50 is a milestone, a wake-up call,
a reminder of everything you
haven't tasted yet and more so,
the possibility of finding yourself
just in time to act on who you are
and what you want.

— *D. A. Wolf*

Now is the time to become a myth.

— *Diane Von Furstenberg*

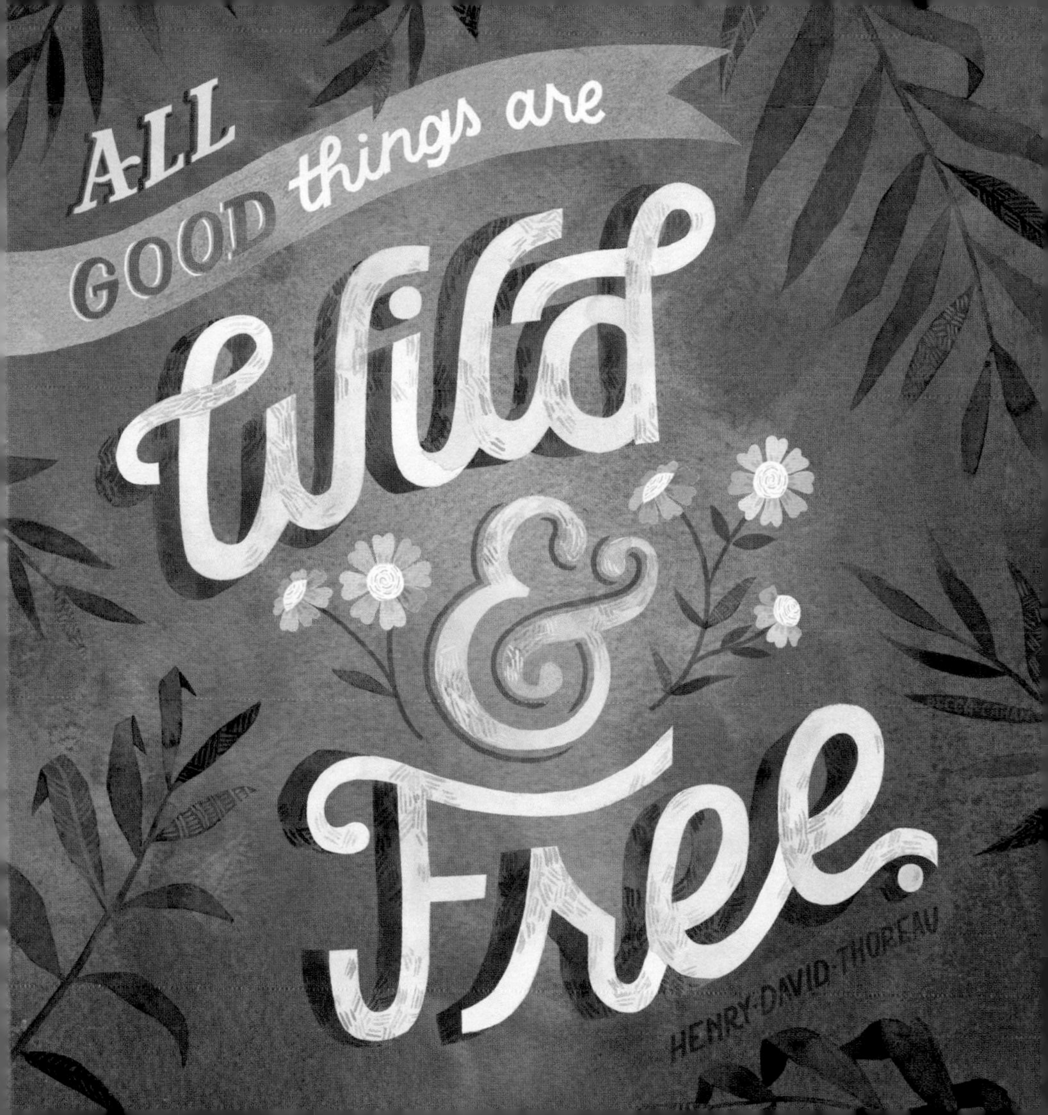
ALL GOOD things are
Wild
&
Free.
HENRY·DAVID·THOREAU

You're not fifty – you're five perfect 10s!

— *Author Unknown*

Time is the coin of your life.
It is the only coin you have, and only
you can determine how it will be spent.
Be careful lest you let other people
spend it for you.

— *Carl Sandburg*